A Little Bit of Advice for
Self-Publishers

A Little Bit of Advice for
Self-Publishers

Vinnie Kinsella

Paper Chain
Book Publishing Services LLC

Portland, Oregon

A Little Bit of Advice for Self-Publishers
Paper Chain Book Publishing Services, Portland, Oregon
paperchainbps.com

Earlier versions of Appendixes A, E, and F appeared in the Indigo Editing & Publications
newsletter.

The version of "Where My Books Go" that appears at the start of this book is taken from
the 1892 edition of *Irish Fairy Tales*, by W. B. Yeats.

Editing by Susan DeFreitas.

ISBN: 978-0-692-65226-8
LCCN: 2016903274

Where My Books Go

All the words that I gather,
    And all the words that I write,
Must spread out their wings untiring,
    And never rest in their flight,
Till they come where your sad, sad heart is,
    And sing to you in the night,
Beyond where the waters are moving,
    Storm darkened or starry bright.

—W. B. YEATS

Contents

Introduction

There's no one right way to self-publish. If there were, there wouldn't be so many how-to books, blogs, and videos on the subject! Google *self-publishing* and see for yourself; the number of resources available is overwhelming. The world doesn't need another how-to guide, and neither do you. So I'm not offering you one. Instead, I'm offering you the little bits of advice I find many authors need at the start of their self-publishing journey, regardless of which how-to guide they decide to follow.

I was fortunate to have earned my master's degree from one of the few universities in the United States that has a book publishing program, Portland State University. There I learned the ins and outs of book editing, book design and production, book marketing and sales, and publication management. This type of education is not made readily available to most authors, even ones who study writing academically. Why would it be? Writing programs are rightly focused on the craft of writing, not the business of publishing. Aside from what they've picked up in a few talks on crafting query letters and book proposals or pitching to agents, most authors lack insight into the world of book creation. This puts many authors who choose self-publishing at a disadvantage, as they likely don't know what they don't know about the process—or even where to begin.

When I began work as a freelance book editor and designer over a decade ago, I didn't set out to help self-published authors. But as the tools for self-publishing became more accessible to authors, I quickly found myself in the role of consultant to clients who wanted to pick my brain about how publishing worked. I was happy to offer my advice because I wanted them to have the best books they possibly could.

Over the years, I have found that many of my clients ask the same questions about the choices they need to make when publishing their books. In responding, I've offered certain key bits of advice. Some advice, such as seeing your cover as a marketing tool, helps give you a framework for decision making at various points in the process. Other advice, such as giving yourself permission to have a meltdown, helps you keep your bearings when things get rough along the way. This book contains the most oft-repeated pieces of advice I give to clients.

Taking your book from manuscript to finished project is an exciting and often stressful process. If my little bits of advice help you in any way, I'd love to hear from you. Reach out to me with your success stories at vinnie@paperchainbps.com.

Happy publishing!
Vinnie Kinsella

Before You Commit

Set Your Own Measure of Success

Success has no standard measure. For some authors, success means making it onto a national bestsellers list. For other authors, it means having just one person they don't know buying and reading their book. As a self-published author, you have the privilege of defining success on your own terms. Before you delve into the process of self-publishing, take the time to set your own measure of success by filling in the blank in the following sentence: I will consider my book successful if _____. Once you have that measure in mind, it will help guide you through the many decisions you will have to make during the publishing process. When faced with a difficult choice about your book's publication, ask which option betters your chances of achieving the success you hope for.

Be Honest about Your Writing

Some authors who've grown exasperated trying to publish traditionally turn to self-publishing after receiving one too many rejection letters from agents and publishers. Choosing self-publishing for this reason can be dangerous if it's rooted in ego (it's one of the two iffy motives for self-publishing I discuss in Appendix A). Before throwing up your hands and saying "I'm tired of this! I'm self-publishing!" take a sober look at what these agents and publishers are saying. If your book isn't ready for traditional publication, perhaps you shouldn't consider it ready for any sort of publication. If you're not sure it's ready, hire an editor to honestly critique your manuscript. The cost of the critique is a small price to pay to find out how much work will really be required to produce a book that's fit for bookstore shelves.

Learn the Publishing Process Before You Undergo It

Gaining an overview of the entire publishing process before you undergo it will help you make better decisions about how to prioritize your time, money, and energy. It will also help reduce surprises along the way. Don't jump into the publishing waters without knowing where the stream will carry you. To help you out, I've added a brief overview of the publishing process to the back of this book (see Appendix B).

Make Your Own Self-Publishing Package

Many authors choose to work with a self-publishing company that offers all-in-one self-publishing packages designed to make it easy to edit, produce, distribute, and sell their books. This can be a low-stress way for you to publish your book; however, your options with these companies are limited. For example, if you want a book cover with French flaps (those lovely flaps that mimic hardback dust jackets on paperback covers), you're not likely going to find a company that offers that option as part of a self-publishing package. The more customization you want, the harder it will be to find a package that will suit you. The good news is, you still have options!

It's entirely possible for you to design your own package using multiple service providers. For example, you can contract your own freelance editors, book designers, and publicists; work with a printer who can produce those wonderful French flaps; and use a fulfillment service to deliver your books to those who buy them.

A more customized book will require extra time and effort to produce, but if it's your dream to have your book a certain way, it's worth it. After all, what's the point of self-publishing if you don't get to have it your way?

Choose Wisely the Company You Keep

If you work with a self-publishing company, your book is affiliated with that company for better or for worse. If the company you publish through is disreputable, this could hurt you. Some book reviewers might refuse to review your book, and some bookstores might refuse to carry it on principle, not wanting to deal with a bad company. Before you commit to a company, do a bit of research on its reputation online. Find out what other authors have to say about the company you are considering. If you want to get your book into a particular bookstore, ask that bookstore about their policy on acquiring self-published books. Many of these policies will flat out state which companies they won't buy books from.

Read Your Contract

If you are using a self-publishing company to produce your book, be sure to read your contract thoroughly before you sign it. Find out what you own and what you don't own. If you ever want to part with the company and release your book another way, you might find it difficult to do so if you don't own the rights to your book's interior and cover (or can't obtain the rights to them without paying a hefty fee). Without those, you'll have to start all over again with the design process—and pay for it all over again too. If you are at all confused by the contract, don't sign it until all your questions are answered satisfactorily. If you don't like the terms of the contract, move on to another company with more favorable terms.

For an excellent primer on understanding self-publishing contracts, I recommend Mark Levine's book *The Fine-Print of Self-Publishing*, which also functions like a *Consumer Reports* for self-publishing companies.

Take Full Responsibility for Your Book's Quality

The publisher is ultimately responsible for a book's quality. That means when you self-publish, quality control rests on your shoulders. If you decide not to work with an editor and then readers complain about the lack of editing in your book, that's on you. If you publish an ebook without doing a quality check of the files before putting it up for sale, you are to blame if readers express frustration over the file's formatting. I say this not to scare you into becoming a perfectionist, but to empower you to remain in control of every step in the process. Always keep the quality of your final product in mind as you consider all your options. For the parts of the process you are giving up control over, make sure to work with reputable service providers who will guarantee their work—and regardless of their reputability, check their work. Self-publishers who take on the responsibility of quality control will have books they can be proud of; those who don't will have no one else to blame if their books disappoint.

Getting the Ball Rolling

Invest in Your Content First

When your budget is limited, it can be tempting to cut your costs by either not hiring an editor at all or hiring one with cheap rates but questionable credentials. This is a mistake. The value of your book is not in its packaging but in its content. If you have a small budget, you'd be better off hiring an editor first and then waiting to produce your book until you are able to save up more money. If you don't work to bring your content to its full potential with the help of an objective eye, the time and money you spend on production and marketing will be largely wasted. Sure, people might buy your book because it has a beautiful cover, but if they find fault with the book's content, they won't recommend it to others (or worse, tell them to avoid it). Word of mouth sustains sales after the initial marketing splash is over. Since word of mouth is driven by satisfied readers, it is your responsibility to give them reason to speak well of your writing.

Define Your Book's Audience Early On

Many people think defining a book's audience matters mostly at the marketing stage. In reality it matters much sooner than that. Because readers have expectations about the books they read within their favorite genres, book editors need to know who the audience is so that they can help you meet their expectations. Similarly, book designers need to know how to make your book fit aesthetically with others like yours (see Appendix E). Before you begin the self-publishing process, you should be able to answer the following question: who will want to read this book? Be specific with your answer. Not everyone will want to read your book, but a group of people will. Work toward reaching that group throughout every stage of the process.

Approach Freelancers Early

When it comes time for you to hire freelancers (be they editors, book designers, publicists, web designers, or anything else), approach the ones you want early on. Freelancers tend to book their projects weeks (sometimes months) in advance. If you wait too long to get into their pipelines, you might not get to work with the ones you want to. Worse than that, you might also have to pay extra to hire another one to do a rush job.

Work with an Honest-to-Goodness Book Editor

Trained book editors do much more than just clean up your typos. They enhance your book through the application of established industry standards (for most of the book-publishing industry, these standards are established in *The Chicago Manual of Style*). Book editors know what readers expect in both content and writing style, and they edit accordingly. They also edit with an objective eye. Unlike your good-at-spelling-and-grammar friend who might edit your book as a favor—and tell you it's great to spare your feelings—an editor will tell you when your writing fails (in a kind way, of course). Working with a skilled editor is so important that even the most qualified editors wouldn't dream of publishing a book of their own without first hiring another editor.

For tips on how to find an editor, see Appendix D.

Work with an Honest-to-Goodness Book Designer

Book designers offer a specialized skill set that extends beyond simply putting your manuscript into a book format. A skilled interior designer fusses over every letter, punctuation mark, word, and line of text to make sure your book is a visual pleasure for the reader. These professionals know such things as exactly how many end-of-line hyphens a reader will endure in a row, which typefaces are best for different kinds of books, and how wide to set the margins on the page to make room for note-takers and people with big thumbs. Similarly, a good cover designer will know how to make your book send the right message to readers (see page 26). Yes, it is entirely possible for you to put your book into a printable and book-like format on your own, but contracting a trained designer can mean the difference between a book that's passable, though still giving off a self-published vibe, and a book that is indistinguishable in appearance from a traditionally published book.

Set a Realistic Release Date

Just because you can produce and release a book in less than a week doesn't mean you should. If you want the final product to be high quality, and if you want it to sell well, you need to build in enough time for editing, design, and prerelease marketing. To avoid making hurried and costly decisions, give yourself ample time to produce your book. I recommend a minimum of eight months from the time you start editing.

Your Book's Final Form

Produce Both Print and Digital Versions

If your book is suitable for both print and digital formats (and most are), there's no reason to go with only one or the other. Today's technology allows for the cost-effective production of both. When you have both, your book becomes available to more readers. So why limit yourself to just one sales stream? However, if you must limit yourself to one format for financial reasons, choose the format your readers are most likely to access, not the one you prefer as a reader.

Read an Ebook for the Sake of Reading an Ebook

If you are reading the ebook version of this book, kudos to you! You've completed your homework and can move on to my next piece of advice. If you are reading the paperback version of this book, pay attention: regardless of your opinion about ebooks, you need to be aware of how readers experience them if you plan to release one. The experience of reading an ebook differs from that of reading a print book in many ways. To understand those differences and how they might impact your book, the best thing you can do is experience them yourself. If you have never read an ebook, pick one to read from start to finish, preferably one in your genre. Take note of what you did and didn't like about the experience. You may never read another ebook again, but at least you'll be aware enough of how they work to think about how readers of ebooks will encounter your content, which may alert you to possible problems between versions of your book.

For more information on quality ebook formatting, see Appendix F.

Properly Prepare Your Files

Book designers often have to spend a lot of time cleaning up the files authors send them. Fixing improperly formatted Microsoft Word files and low-quality images can really slow down the process and add to the cost of your design. To put less strain on your designer (and your wallet), ask them upfront how they prefer to have files prepared. If you don't know in advance who your designer will be, you're safe following the file preparation guidelines spelled out in *The Chicago Manual of Style*.

See Your Book's Cover as a Marketing Tool

Your book's cover should send a message to readers that says, "This is the book you are looking for." If you pick your cover based solely on what you find aesthetically pleasing, you can easily send the wrong message, thus mismarketing your book. If a science fiction novel is adorned only with watercolor images of beautiful flowers and hummingbirds, its target audience will overlook it. Why? Because it says, "I'm a poetry anthology." Before you pick your cover, examine how other books in your genre are presented. Think of how they look as the dress code for yours.

Test Your Cover's Visual Cues

Because your book cover is designed to catch a reader's attention, it's important to test its visual cues. Before you commit to a cover, run both a ten-foot test and a two-inch test.

For the ten-foot test, stand at least ten feet away from your cover and ask if it would catch your eye in a bookstore from that distance. Would you walk across the room to examine it closer? If yes, then it passed the test.

For the two-inch test, shrink the cover down to about two inches to approximate how it will appear when scrolling through an online bookstore. Ask if it would catch your eye enough to make you click on the image to learn more about the book. As with the ten-foot test, if the answer is yes, it passed.

It can be tricky to create a cover that passes both tests, but it's not impossible. If you find that your cover can pass only one, make sure it passes the test that best targets the environment in which most of your readers will buy their books.

Keep Your Printing Costs Low

Math alert! When working with bookstores, you must factor in both wholesale and retail prices. The wholesale price (the price at which you sell your book to retailers) is typically 45 percent of the retail price (the price at which bookstores sell the book to readers).* That means if your book's retail price is $15.00, you would sell it to retailers for a wholesale price of $6.75. Out of that $6.75 comes your print cost. What's left is your profit. If it costs you $6.50 to print the book (a high price I made up for the purpose of illustration), you've made only $0.25. That's terrible! To make more money, you'll either need to set the wholesale price much higher (a bad idea, since that means also upping the retail price) or lower your printing cost. The second option is by far the better of the two. If you are using a print on demand service (which most self-publishers do), a good rule of thumb is that you should pay no more than $0.02 per page for a standard black-and-white paperback. Anything more than that is going to hurt your bottom line.

* This is a bit simplified, as it assumes there's a book wholesaler in the mix, which is typical for print on demand services. You are technically selling the book to the wholesaler at 45 percent of the retail price. The wholesaler in turn sells it to bookstores for 60 percent of the retail price. This is important to note because if you are working directly with bookstores without going through a wholesaler, you might be able to negotiate a deal with bookstores in which your wholesale price is 50 to 60 percent of the retail price instead of 45 percent.

Marketing and Sales

Release Your Book in the Right Season

In addition to setting a realistic release date (see page 20), you also want to set a release date that suits the book's content. There's an obvious reason why holiday books come out in the fall: they need to be on sale in time for the holidays. Before releasing your book, research if there's a time of year in which comparable titles are typically released. If there is, consider releasing your book then. This might mean delaying your book's release several months longer than you planned on, but it's far better to do so than to have your book come out at a time when it has little relevance to readers.

Promote Your Book before It Comes Out

If you put off promoting your book until after it comes out, you could miss out on a lot of opportunities. Many publicity streams are accessible only to authors with forthcoming titles. For example, trade magazines that target bookstores generally accept books for review before they are released but not after. The longer you wait to promote your book, the less publicity you're likely to get. If you don't have a plan in place to start promoting your book before its release, delay your release and make one.

Partner Up

If the content of your book raises awareness of a particular cause, there may be affiliated organizations interested in promoting your work. If, for example, your book focuses on sloth conservation, any number of sloth conservation organizations would likely share your book in their newsletters. If your book doesn't raise awareness for a particular cause, you can still partner with an organization by donating a portion of your book's sales to a nonprofit you support. Doing so gives them reason to promote your book, since the more copies of your book you sell, the more they will benefit. It also gives people who support that organization a reason to buy your book.

Have a Website, Even If It's Simple

Having a website adds validity to your marketing endeavors. The good news is that yours doesn't have to be extravagant. All readers expect is a place where they can learn about your book (including where to buy it) and about you as the author. Many web designers offer services to fit any budget, so don't hesitate to approach one. As long as you include the basics, you're well covered.

Name Your Publishing Company

Although the stigma against self-published books has largely faded for most readers, some will still hesitate to knowingly purchase a self-published book. Fortunately, you don't have to disclose to potential readers that your book is self-published. When you self-publish a book, you are going into business for yourself. Give your business its own name, logo, website—the works! If you do this well, the only people who will know you self-published are the people you choose to tell.

Don't think it will work? Answer this question for me: who published the last book you read? If you are like most readers, you have no clue. That's because most readers are only aware of a book's publisher if it somehow sticks out to them. Unless you are using your face as your logo, it's unlikely the majority of readers will recognize that your publishing company is run by the only author it publishes.

Have an Elevator Pitch for Your Book

The moment you tell others that you've published a book, they're going to ask you what it's about. Take a page from any Marketing 101 textbook and be prepared to offer them an articulate, thirty-second description of your book (an elevator pitch). When you do, you come across as both passionate about your work and skilled in the art of communication. Who wouldn't want to buy a book from someone like that?

Market Where Your Readers Are

Sometimes marketing your book in the conventional places can be a waste of time. Social media updates, bookstore signings, and book reviews are only helpful if your readers find out about books in those ways. If your readers are more likely to find out about your book at a flea market or a track meet, those are the places you need to market your book. This is another benefit of defining your audience early on (see page 16). Once you know who your readers are, it's a lot easier to figure out where they find out about books.

Play by the Bookstore's Rules

If you want your book sold in bookstores (be they physical or online), you need to play by their rules. Each one has policies for how books are acquired, and they are not the same for each store. For example, if your book does not have a distributor, chain bookstores aren't as likely to carry it; however, your local independent stores might sell it on consignment without a distributor. Before you approach a bookstore about carrying your book, find out how it acquires the books it sells. This information is often available on the store's website. If a bookstore's rules prevent them from acquiring your book, don't waste their time trying to convince them to take it.

Caring for Your Publisher (You)

Know That Someone Will Dislike Your Book

Online reader reviews can be wonderful for your book when they are positive. But there is a dark side to these reviews. Unlike reviews by established book reviewers, who have set standards by which they assess books, everyday readers have arbitrary standards. This is why you regularly see negative reviews of books by people who haven't even read them, but simply dislike the author's subject matter. As your book gains exposure, it's almost inevitable that someone will post a negative review of your book online, and possibly just to be malicious. You can't control that. When that happens, your job is not to defend your work or try to change that person's opinion—your job is to take a deep breath, remember the praise your work has received from others, and move on. Criticism is part of a published writer's life. You have to take it in stride and trust that other readers will see through the naysayer's bias.

Be Okay with Okay

At some point in the self-publishing process, you will have to make compromises. Before this point comes, it helps to know where you are willing to bend. For example, you might start out intending to release your book as a hardback as well as a paperback, but you might find out in the process that you can't afford to do it both ways. If you already decided that you'd be okay with just a paperback, you lose nothing when circumstances force you to pass on the hardback. When setting up your publishing plan (see Appendix C), it helps to prioritize your options and identify which ones are desirable but not absolutely required. It's also important to keep your vision for success (see page 5) in mind so that you can make compromises that won't steer you away from your goal.

Give Yourself Permission to Have a Meltdown

Being both the author and publisher of your book can be stressful, especially if you've never published before. You will find yourself overwhelmed at some point. When you do, go ahead and have a meltdown. It's best not to let your stress stay bottled up if you want to continue with a clear head. Do whatever it takes to let it all out: curl up into a ball on the floor and cry, scream into your pillow, curse the sky. As a matter of practice, I tell authors I work with that they get one free meltdown when working with me, so they better make it a good one. They always laugh when I say that...until they have the meltdown.

Don't Let Surprises Derail You

No matter how solid your publishing plan is, no matter how prepared for the process you think you are, unexpected complications will arise. It could be anything from the artist whose work you planned to use for the cover denying you permission to use his art to the proofreader you contracted fleeing the country the day she was supposed to start working with you. When something like this happens, don't let it derail you. Chances are, this unexpected complication won't be that big of a deal to work around. There is always a plan B to be found. You might need to have a meltdown before you can find it (see the previous tip), but you will find it.

Stop to Catch Your Breath

Once you commit to self-publishing, you've got your work cut out for you. Somewhere between making decisions about what content to cut, what fonts to use in your interior, what price to set your book at, and the myriad other decisions you'll have to make, you can forget about your own needs. As difficult as it might seem to take time for yourself, it's really one of the most productive things you can do. When you give yourself some space to breathe, you can return to the mound of work with renewed vigor. Schedule a day trip, enroll in an exercise class, go to a café and read—do whatever it takes for you to relax. The pile of work will seem far less mountainous if you step away from it for even a short while.

Appendix A

Reasons to Self-Publish (Two Good, Two Iffy)

Good Reason Number One: Profits Are Secondary to Getting Your Message Out

If all you want is for people to hear what you have to say, self-publishing can be a great option for you. Without the need to generate profits for a publisher, you are free to give your book away or price it low in the hope of spreading your message. Authors who self-publish for this reason can benefit from a more relaxed process because they aren't worried about the financial success of the book. Success for them is measured in impact, not profits.

Good Reason Number Two: You Have Direct Access to Your Own Market

An author who writes the definitive history of the small coastal town she lives in is likely better off as a self-published author than one who writes a novel set in the same town. Why? Because the history writer already knows the majority of her readers and how to make them aware of her book, since they are members of her community. The novelist has a broader audience to reach, since there are millions of fiction readers out there. She might be better off seeking publication with an established fiction publisher that already reaches her audience. If you, like the history author, have a strong connection to your audience, you have good reason to self-publish.

Iffy Reason Number One: You're Tired of Rejection from Agents and Publishers

There are far more people wanting to publish traditionally than there are companies to publish them. If you are one of those authors who keeps receiving rejection letters, thumbing your nose at the traditional model might seem like a viable way to avoid further frustration. But don't be rash. Without knowing for sure if it's the content itself or just bad luck keeping you from getting published, you run the risk of releasing a half-baked book readers themselves reject. Before you set out on your own, find out for sure why the rejection letters keep coming (see page 6).

Iffy Reason Number Two: You Hope Publishing Your Own Book Will Help It Get Discovered by a Publisher or Agent

It's true that some agents and publishers notice when readers respond positively to a self-published book. However, the odds of getting your self-published book picked up by a publisher are not in your favor. Even if your book is a hit with readers, that doesn't guarantee an open door to traditional publishing. If you enter into self-publishing without the ability to find contentment with your successes in that realm, you're better off avoiding it altogether. It's better to commit to self-publishing when you know you can be happy with your choice regardless of whether or not your book gets published another way.

Appendix B

The Publishing Process in a Nutshell

Regardless of whether you publish your book traditionally or self-publish it, the process of getting your book into the hands of the reader involves the same steps: editing, design, production, distribution, marketing, and sales and fulfillment. Let's take a quick look at each step.

Editing is the process of ensuring that what the reader comprehends lines up with what you intended to put on the page. This can happen at the content level and at the writing mechanics level. For example, if you intend for your main character to be optimistic and inspiring but he comes across to readers as naïve and annoying, something went amiss in the process of getting the character out of your head and onto the page. A good developmental editor (sometimes called a content editor) can work with you to flesh out the character, identify places where the writing undermines your intentions for him, and help you convey the vital information readers need in order to understand the character the way you do. At the writing mechanics level, a line editor (sometimes called a copyeditor) ensures that when you intend for your main character to *defiantly* enter the room, he's not *definitely* entering the room.

Design is the process of taking what you've written and setting it up to be turned into forms that will be accessible to your reader. In terms of books, this generally involves laying out your manuscript in book form for print, converting the text into ebook form, and designing a cover for the book. The design process largely takes place after the editing is complete, but parts of it can take place while the book is still in editing, such as designing the cover and deciding on the basics of the print book (trim size, font choices, paper color and thickness, etc.). After the book has been laid out and before it enters production, there is often a round of proofreading, the level of editing focused solely on correcting errors.

Production is the process of taking what the designer set up and fixing it into its final physical form. This generally means printing and binding the book; however, other forms of a book might need to go through a production process as well. For example, an audiobook version being delivered to listeners through physical forms such as CDs and thumb drives will also need production.

Distribution is the process of taking all accessible forms of the book and making them available to retailers. This could mean working with an actual book distributor to reach retailers or working directly with booksellers yourself. Many print on demand companies offer basic distribution services to help you reach booksellers, and several of the larger bookstore chains and online retailers have their own programs for selling self-published books.

Marketing, defined broadly, is the process of making readers aware of your book. This can include publicity campaigns, advertising, social media campaigns, blog tours, and a myriad of other strategies. Marketing can begin at the start of the publishing process, and generally is most effective before the book's release (see page 32).

Sales is the process of selling the book in all of its forms to readers. You can do this in many ways: through online stores, through brink-and-mortar stores, directly through your website, and in person. Most sales services available to self-publishers also include fulfillment services, but keep in mind that if you sell directly, you will also need a plan to fulfill your customer's orders. You are not limited to one sales model, and in fact are wise to use multiple models at once. The sales process can begin before the book is officially released through presales.

Appendix C

Developing a Self-Publishing Plan

Successful self-publishing begins with a plan. Before you commit to publishing your own writing, you should be able to answer the following questions.

1. What is your measure of success for your book (see page 5)?

2. As an independent publisher, will you be conducting business as a sole proprietor, or will you be conducting business through an LLC, corporation, or nonprofit organization?

3. Who will edit your book?

4. In which of the following formats will you release your book?
    *   Paperback
    *   Hardback
    *   Ebook
    *   Audiobook
    *   All of the above

5. Who will design your book's cover?

6. Who will lay out your book's interior?

7. Who will handle your ebook conversion?

8. How do you intend to print your book?
   - Traditional offset printing
   - Digital short-run printing
   - Print on demand

9. In which of the following ways will you sell your book?
   - Through a personal website
   - Through online retailers
   - Through independent bookstores
   - Through chain bookstores
   - All of the above

10. If selling through a personal website, how do you plan to fulfill your orders?

11. When do you intend to release your book?

12. Do you intend to take presale orders of your book before the release date?

13. Do you have a marketing strategy to reach your book's audience?

14. Will the marketing strategy be implemented, at least in part, before the book's release?

Appendix D

Finding an Editor

Perhaps the single most important relationship you will forge in the publishing process is the author/editor relationship. But if you have never worked with an editor before, finding one can be a challenge. To help you find the editor that's best for you, here are a few basic tips on how to begin your hunt.

Ask for Recommendations from Other Authors

The easiest way to find an editor you'll love is to find one other authors already love. The author/editor relationship thrives on trust, specifically the trust an author has that their editor will make them look their best. Ask around and find out which editors the authors in your area already trust. Use those names as your shortlist of possible candidates.

Look for an Editor Who Specializes in Your Genre

Although skilled editors have what it takes to work in a wide range of genres, most specialize. The benefit of working with an editor who specializes in your genre is that he or she brings more to the table than just a good grasp of language. An editor who specializes is aware of trends in a specific genre, which authors have set the gold standard for their genre, and what readers of that genre will expect from your book. That added industry knowledge will only enhance the work your editor does.

Ask for an Editor's Credentials

Did your editor of interest study editing formally in college?

Does she have an editing certification from a reputable program? Can she provide you with a list of books she's worked on? An editor with strong credentials will be happy to share them with you, so don't be afraid to ask.

Ask for a Sample Edit of Your Work

One of the best ways to decide if an editor is right for you is to have the editor edit a sample of your work. Upon reviewing the sample edit, you should almost immediately know if the editor is capable of offering the help you need. If the sample makes you think, "I didn't know my writing could be so good," you've likely found a keeper. If the sample feels like it did more damage than good, or if for some reason the editor won't provide you with a sample edit, walk away.

Don't Let Cost Be Your Only Deciding Factor

Good editors are worth what they charge. Cheap editors are also worth what they charge. If an editor has rates well below what is standard in the market, that's a red flag. That's usually a sign of lack: lack of skill, lack of repeat clients, lack of professionalism. Cost should be a factor when choosing an editor, but it shouldn't be the first thing you consider. Focus first on finding a skilled editor, then talk about rates. If you approach it the other way around, you'll likely end up paying more, as you'll have to hire a second editor to make up for your first editor's lack (an unfortunately common occurrence among self-published authors).

Trust Your Gut

I can't stress this point enough. As stated before, the author/editor relationship is based on trust. This means you have to click with your editor. If you have any sense that you won't work well with an editor, even a very skilled one, don't. You should feel good about the editor you choose.

Appendix E

Avoiding the Self-Published Look

In the same way that poorly edited content can turn readers away, so can a poorly designed book. Why? Because the book itself is a marketing tool. If the book appears poorly constructed, readers will associate the poor craftsmanship of the book with the writing it contains and hesitate to buy it. This doesn't have to be your book's fate, though. By avoiding the biggest reasons why a book's design fails, your book will not fall victim to the so-called self-published look.

There are two main ways a book's design can do more harm than good. The first is that the interior lacks strong readability. The second is that the cover sends the wrong message.

The Readability of Your Book's Interior
In the context of book design, readability refers to how easy it is for readers to visually interact with the text. The more effort put into making the text readable, the easier it is for readers to keep turning pages without needing to pause because of eyestrain. Here is a simple way to test if a book's interior has been laid out with strong readability in mind. Look for hyphens along the right-hand margin of several pages. If you don't see any, that likely means your book was designed without strong attention to readability. Those hyphens are a result of a trained typesetter breaking words at the end of lines to achieve optimal spacing, ensuring there are neither too few nor too many characters on a line. When these hyphens are absent, it means the person responsible for laying out your

book's interior wasn't using one of the most reliable tools in the typesetter's toolkit.

To increase a book's readability, a typesetter must consider several factors: font choice, leading (space between lines), kerning (space between letters and characters), hyphenation and justification (how lines are broken along the margin), line length, and the number of lines per page. If any of these factors aren't considered, readability is lessened.

Most self-publishers know little about formatting book interiors for readability. And why should they? They're writers, not typesetters. Although many self-publishing companies offer basic interior layout services or templates for book layout, few offer more than a quick-and-dirty approach to the task. The book might be technically readable, but it won't have the same level of readability as a professionally laid out book.

Regardless of whether or not you contract a book designer to layout your book, it's a good idea to educate yourself on the basics of readability. Round out your writing bookshelf with books on the topics of both typography and book design. Knowing the basics will give you a way to assess the quality of your book's interior and help you avoid releasing a book readers must strain their eyes to read.

Your Cover's Message

Book buyers are drawn to covers with strong messages and repelled by covers with weak or misleading messages. Publishers of genre fiction know this well. If a romance novel's cover looks like a poetry anthology cover, romance readers will walk right past it in the bookstore. They are looking for visual clues that say, "I'm a romance novel. Buy me!" When those clues aren't there, the book will be ignored by its target audience—even if its cover is beautiful. This is why books within a genre tend to have similar covers.

It doesn't take much to send the right message to readers. Take, for example, the first edition of Cormac McCarthy's Pulitzer Prize winner, *The Road*. When it was released, the cover was all black with the author's name in gray and the title in red. There was no image, just a black background with some gray and red letters. It was simple and to the point. That's all that was needed to send a message to readers that the story was a dark and desolate tale written by one of America's best-known authors.

If you want readers to notice your book on a shelf, shift your thinking from "How do I want my cover to look?" to "What marketing message do I want my cover to convey?" After that question is answered, you can then make aesthetic decisions that support your message.

To Do It Yourself or Not to Do It Yourself?

Given all the time you spent perfecting your writing, you owe it to your book to present it in the best way possible within your budget. Many of the mistakes made that harm a self-published book's design are usually made by authors doing all the design work themselves to save money. It's not that such authors are incompetent; it's just that they often have limited knowledge of the tools the pros use. If you decide to hire a professional, I would offer almost the same advice I offer about finding an editor in Appendix D. In fact, you can pretty much just swap *designer* in for *editor* in most spots and call it Appendix D.2. If you opt to do your own design work, commit to first learning all you can about book design fundamentals so that you can be aware of and avoid the pitfalls of the self-published look. And no matter what, always keep in mind that the quality control falls on you (see page 11).

Appendix F

Making Sure Your Ebook Rocks

As a lifelong bibliophile, I took little interest in ebooks when they made a splash in the late aughts. To me, a book was a physical object; therefore, an ebook was simply not a book. The idea of reading an entire story on a screen like Captain Picard on *Star Trek: The Next Generation* seemed unnatural, almost vulgar. However, I knew it was inevitable that one day a client's project would force me to deal with ebooks. So I bought a Kindle for work and challenged myself to read just one book on it in its entirety, a challenge I now make to all self-published authors (see page 24).

The book I chose was *The Hunger Games*, which I had yet to read at that point, and which had not yet been turned into a movie. As I began clicking through the pages (let's not call it turning), the wonders of ebooks opened up to me: instant gratification when I wanted a new book, an extensive library always with me, and no more paperbacks I had no intention of rereading taking up shelf space. I became a fan of the experience (a bit to my own dismay), and in less than a week, I had downloaded and devoured the entirety of Suzanne Collins's dystopian young adult series.

Having become an ebook lover myself—and now also being an ebook designer—I can say with assurance that there are such things as bad ebooks. I'm not referring to content (bad content is bad content in any book format). I'm referring to the actual formatting of the ebook. So, in the interest of making my musings about ebooks relevant to you, I offer my top four ways to make sure your ebook rocks.

Format Your Ebook Properly

In some ways, ebook design can be more complex than print design. When formatting an ebook, you must consider such things as accessibility for disabled readers, compatibility across multiple devices, and limitations to the publisher's control over display options. Good standards in digital publishing are so important that there is an entire organization devoted to developing these standards, the International Digital Publishing Forum (idpf.org).

Avid readers of ebooks are quickly frustrated when their digital books are formatted poorly. If you are going to offer an ebook, don't just run it through some conversion software and hope for the best. Hire a person who knows how to properly code a book for readability and maximum compatibility across devices. Self-publishing companies often offer quick-and-dirty ebook conversions that get the job done, but these services don't always yield good results, especially with nonfiction books containing lots of design elements (such as block quotes, lists, callouts, and the like). For most books, paying the extra cost of working with a person or company that guarantees a human quality check of the files is worth it to avoid complaints about the ebook's formatting from your readers.

Take Full Advantage of Interactive Features

Does your book have URLs in the reference section? Make them clickable in the ebook. Does your book have footnotes? Make sure the referents and notes are hyperlinked. Take advantage of an ebook's interactive features in every way you can, as this will make the experience richer for your readers. It will also keep them from complaining when they see ways the ebook could be interactive but isn't, which is a pet peeve of those who prefer ebooks to print books.

Accommodate for Content That Works for the Print Version but Not the Ebook Version

If your print book invites readers to fill out a worksheet on a page, you should be aware that readers of your ebook won't have that ability. To assist them, you could offer them a link to workbook pages on your website that they can download, print off, and fill out on their own (much like I did in Appendix C). As you edit your book, be on the lookout for any material that doesn't consider the needs of both print and ebook readers. With a little bit of planning, you can find ways to make the material work for both sets of readers.

Proofread the Dang Thing

Most often, an ebook is created after the print book is laid out. During the conversion process, new errors can easily be introduced. Although these are typically errors in coding that result in things such as odd paragraph breaks, they can still frustrate readers. Just taking the time to click through all the content once can reveal problems that would otherwise get passed on to the readers. Unfortunately, many self-publishers skip this step because they aren't ebook readers themselves. Don't let your reading preference be an excuse to offer an inferior experience for readers with a different preference. For their sakes, check the ebook for problems from beginning to end.

Further Reading

As I mentioned in the introduction to this book, there is no shortage of how-to guides for self-publishers. To keep this section simple, I'm offering you just a short list of guides I know will be worth your money. Some will help you with developing your publishing plan. Others will offer good insight into parts of the process unfamiliar to most authors.

APE: Author, Publisher, Entrepreneur—How to Publish a Book, by Guy Kawasaki and Shawn Welch

Book Design, by Andrew Haslam

The Fine Print of Self-Publishing: A Primer on Contracts, Printing Costs, Royalties, Distribution, E-Books, and Marketing, by Mark Levine

The Non-Designer's Design Book, by Robin Williams

The Self-Publisher's Ultimate Resource Guide: Every Indie Author's Essential Directory—To Help You Prepare, Publish, and Promote Professional Looking Books, by Joel Friedlander and Betty Kelly Sargent

Write. Publish. Repeat.: The No-Luck-Required Guide to Self-Publishing Success, by Sean Platt and Johnny B. Truant

Your First 1000 Copies: The Step-by-Step Guide to Marketing Your Book, by Tim Grahl

About the Author

Vinnie Kinsella's work with books began in the second grade when he and his classmates wrote and illustrated a story about the adventures of an ice-cream-loving giraffe. Years later, in 2006, he earned his master's in writing and publishing from Portland State University. Since then, he has used his skills as an editor, book designer, and publication manager to help hundreds of authors and publishers release quality books into the world. He is currently the owner of Paper Chain Book Publishing Service in Portland, Oregon.

www.ingramcontent.com/pod-product-compliance
Lightning Source LLC
Chambersburg PA
CBHW052017230326
41598CB00078B/3576